RELEASING THE PROPHETIC DESTINY OF A NATION OFFICIAL WORKBOOK

AN INTERCESSOR'S HANDBOOK TO PRAY FOR ALL 50 STATES IN AMERICA

TIM SHEETS   DUTCH SHEETS   CHUCK D. PIERCE

Faith and Flame P.O. Box 310, Shippensburg, PA 17257-0310

This book and all other Faith and Flame's books are available at Christian bookstores and distributors worldwide.

For Worldwide Distribution, Printed in the U.S.A.

Reach us on the Internet: www.faithandflame.com.

ISBN 13 TP: 9780768482355

ISBN 13 eBook: 9780768483161

❋ Created with Vellum

CONTENTS

INTRODUCTION

Welcome to this transformative journey through the powerful messages and declarations in this workbook. As you dive into each chapter, you will encounter profound truths, divine revelations, and actionable steps designed to empower you in your walk with God. This workbook is more than just a collection of teachings; it is a guide to help you align with God's purposes, activate His promises, and see His Kingdom come to earth.

Key Takeaways

Each chapter in this workbook carries a unique message that is essential for understanding God's plan for His people and the nations. Here are the key takeaways from the chapters covered:

1. **Reconnecting to Covenant Roots**: We begin by understanding the importance of reconnecting to our spiritual roots. This foundational step is crucial for entering a God-ordained season of reset. As we reconnect, we position ourselves to receive God's promises and walk in His divine purposes.

2. **Change and Divine Assistance**: We are in a time of significant change, and angel armies are activated to assist us. This chapter emphasizes the role of angels in fulfilling God's plans and the importance of our decrees in mobilizing these heavenly beings.

3. **Glorious Remnant Mobilizing**: A glorious remnant is rising, using their decrees to engage angel armies. By aligning our words with God's will, we activate the power of His promises and see them manifest in our lives and communities.

4. **Days of Awakening and Revival**: We are called to align with Heaven and ask for an acceleration of anointing and outpourings. This chapter focuses on the urgency of revival and the role of angel armies in bringing about this spiritual awakening.

5. **Salvation for America and the Nations**: The declaration that America will be saved extends to all nations. It is a call for global salvation and a reminder that it is time for the fulfillment of God's redemptive plans.

6. **No More Delay**: Revival is now. This chapter stresses the immediacy of God's move and the need for us to be ready and expectant for His intervention in our lives and nation.

7. **Resurrection Life and Unity**: Dry bones will live again, symbolizing new breath and life entering God's people. This unity is essential for standing as a great army, ready to advance His Kingdom.

8. **Healing and Miracles**: Angels are stirring the waters, leading to accelerated healings and miracles. We are called to expect and declare these supernatural interventions in our midst.

9. **Harvest and Prodigals Returning**: The time for harvest is now, with prodigals returning and new converts joining the faith. This chapter highlights the role of angelic assistance in the harvest and the importance of our participation.

10. **Justice and Righteousness**: Justice will prevail over injustice, with the Ekklesia rising

to use their voice and authority. This chapter focuses on the necessity of the church's involvement in societal and cultural transformation.

What to Expect

As you work through this workbook, you will be equipped with tools and insights to:

- **Align with God's Purposes**: Each chapter provides a framework for understanding and aligning with God's will for your life and nation. By aligning your prayers and actions with His plans, you will see His Kingdom come in powerful ways.
- **Activate Angelic Assistance**: Learn how to partner with angel armies through your decrees and prayers. By engaging with these heavenly beings, you will experience divine intervention and support in your endeavors.
- **Mobilize for Revival**: Discover the keys to personal and corporate revival. This workbook will guide you in seeking and experiencing an outpouring of the Holy Spirit that brings transformation and renewal.

- **Stand for Justice and Righteousness**: Be inspired to take a stand for justice in your community and nation. Learn how to use your voice and authority to influence societal and cultural changes that align with God's Kingdom.

- **Experience Supernatural Breakthroughs**: Expect to see healings, miracles, and supernatural breakthroughs as you declare God's promises over your life and circumstances. This workbook provides practical steps to activate these divine interventions.

- **Participate in the Harvest**: Be prepared to engage in the harvest of souls, seeing prodigals return and new believers join the faith. Understand your role in this great mission and how to effectively participate in it.

- **Embrace Your Identity in Christ**: Each chapter reinforces your identity as a child of God, called to reign and rule with Him. Embrace this identity and step into the fullness of what He has called you to be.

Final Thoughts

This workbook is a journey of discovery and empowerment. As you read, reflect, and apply the teachings, you will be transformed and equipped to make a significant impact in your sphere of influence. Remember, you are not alone in this journey. Angel armies are ready to assist you, and the power of God's word is at your disposal.

Commit to this journey with an open heart and a willing spirit. Allow the Holy Spirit to guide you, and be prepared to see God's Kingdom come in unprecedented ways. This is a season of reset, revival, and restoration. Embrace it fully and watch as God does extraordinary things in and through your life.

HOW TO USE THIS WORKBOOK

How to Get the Most Out of This Workbook

Welcome to this comprehensive workbook, designed to guide you through powerful messages, divine revelations, and actionable steps to align with God's purposes. To help you fully engage and receive the maximum benefit, follow these ten key points:

1. Set Aside Dedicated Time for Study

To truly absorb and apply the teachings in this workbook, set aside a specific time each day or week for study. This dedicated time will allow you to focus, reflect, and engage with the material without distractions. Consistency is key to building a strong foundation in understanding and applying the principles discussed.

2. Pray for Guidance and Revelation

Begin each session with prayer, asking the Holy Spirit

to guide you, open your understanding, and reveal the deeper meanings of the messages. Prayer will help you connect with God and prepare your heart to receive His word. It will also enable you to discern how to apply the teachings to your personal life and circumstances.

3. Read Each Chapter Thoroughly

Take your time to read each chapter thoroughly, allowing the words to sink in. Don't rush through the material. Instead, meditate on the key points and reflect on how they relate to your current situation. This deliberate approach will help you grasp the full depth of the teachings and their implications for your life.

4. Reflect on the Word of Encouragement and Bible Verse

Each chapter begins with a word of encouragement and a related Bible verse. Reflect on these words and verses, considering how they speak to your heart and current circumstances. Write down any thoughts or insights that come to mind, and revisit them throughout your study to reinforce the message.

5. Engage with the Reflective Questions

The reflective questions at the end of each chapter are designed to help you internalize the teachings and apply them to your life. Take time to answer each question thoughtfully and honestly. Write your responses in a journal or notebook, and review them periodically to track your spiritual growth and progress.

6. Implement the Actionable Steps

Each chapter includes actionable steps—Cultivate, Equip, and Engage—that provide practical ways to apply the teachings. Make a commitment to follow these steps and integrate them into your daily routine. By taking concrete actions, you will see the teachings come to life and experience real change.

7. Use the Journaling Prompt

Journaling is a powerful tool for reflection and growth. Use the journaling prompts provided at the end of each chapter to record your thoughts, prayers, and experiences. This practice will help you process what you've learned, track your progress, and see how God is working in your life.

8. Review and Reflect Regularly

Periodically review the chapters you have completed, your journal entries, and your responses to the reflective questions. Reflect on the progress you've made and the insights you've gained. This regular review will reinforce the teachings and help you stay on track with your spiritual journey.

9. Share and Discuss with Others

Share what you're learning with a trusted friend, family member, or small group. Discussing the material with others can provide new insights, encouragement, and accountability. It also allows you to learn from the experiences and perspectives of others, enriching your understanding and application of the teachings.

10. Be Open to Transformation

Approach this workbook with an open heart and mind, ready to be transformed by God's word. Be willing to let go of old patterns, beliefs, and behaviors that do not align with His purposes. Embrace the changes that come as you apply the teachings, and trust that God is guiding you towards a deeper relationship with Him and greater effectiveness in His Kingdom.

Detailed Guide to Using Each Chapter Component Chapter Title and Word of Encouragement

- The chapter title gives you an overview of the main theme. Reflect on what the title means to you before diving into the content.
- The word of encouragement sets the tone for the chapter. Let it inspire you and prepare your heart to receive the teaching.

Bible Verse

- Read the Bible verse carefully, considering its context and relevance to the chapter's theme.

- Memorize the verse if possible, and meditate on it throughout your day. Let it become a part of your thought life.

Paragraph Form Summary

- The summary provides a concise overview of the chapter's key points. Use it as a quick reference to recall the main ideas.
- Reflect on how the summary ties into your personal experiences and current spiritual journey.

Reflective Questions

- Answer each question honestly, taking time to think deeply about your responses.
- Use these questions as a tool for self-examination and spiritual growth.

Actionable Steps

- Cultivate: Identify specific areas in your life where you need to grow and take intentional steps to nurture that growth.

- Equip: Seek out resources, knowledge, and skills that will help you implement the teachings. This could involve reading additional materials, attending workshops, or seeking mentorship.
- Engage: Actively apply what you've learned in your daily life. Look for opportunities to practice the principles and make a tangible impact.

Journaling Prompt

- Use the journaling prompt to write down your thoughts, prayers, and reflections.
- Revisit your journal entries regularly to see how you've grown and to remind yourself of God's faithfulness.

CHAPTER 1

THE RIDE

Remember, the journey of intercession and spiritual leadership is not just about reaching a destination but about being faithful to the call. Stand firm in your faith, knowing that God equips those He calls.

"I will give you the keys of the kingdom of heaven, and whatever you bind on earth will be bound in heaven, and whatever you loose on earth will be loosed in heaven." - Matthew 16:19, NKJV

I n the first chapter titled "The Ride," I recount a pivotal moment that laid the groundwork for a significant spiritual mission that would span the entire United States. My journey began with a vivid, compelling **Vision of Riding with Christ** on His white warhorse. This wasn't just an ordinary dream but a powerful image that filled me with both awe and trepidation. It was a clear sign that my spiritual journey was about to intertwine deeply with a divine calling that would affect the entire nation.

As I delve into the details of this nationwide mission, I distinctly remember when the **Call to Action in 2002** was delivered. This directive wasn't just meant for me but also for my fellow spiritual laborer, Chuck Pierce. We were tasked by the Holy Spirit to visit all 50 states. Our mission was clear: to unite intercessors and leaders, pray for spiritual breakthroughs, and ignite a shift towards revival. This was a direct summons from God, marking a decisive path we were to follow, highlighting the seriousness and urgency of our calling.

Going back to 1998, while I was speaking at a conference, I received an **Initial Vision in 1998**. I saw America from a heavenly perspective, observing the nation as if from above, with Christ at the center, ready for battle. This vision served as a forewarning of the spiritual warfare that lay ahead and was an early call to prepare for what was to come. It impressed upon me the importance of spiritual readiness and set the stage for the actions that would follow.

Throughout my journey, I have experienced moments of profound divine interaction, which I refer to as

Dynamic and Intense Divine Interactions. One particularly transformative moment occurred while I was ministering at a conference in Colorado Springs. I felt an overwhelming spiritual weight, leading to a lengthy period of spiritual impartation. These experiences deepened my spiritual resolve and prepared me for the daunting tasks ahead. They reminded me of the intense reality of the spiritual realm and the significant impact of my actions.

My role in the prayer movement and insights into national events often came through **Prophetic Insights on National Matters**. Especially during the presidential elections of 2000, I received significant revelations that shaped my understanding of America's spiritual landscape. These insights directed my prayers and actions, influencing how I led the prayer movement in response to the nation's spiritual needs.

A recurring theme in my narrative is the **Role of Spiritual Authority**. God confirmed that He was entrusting me with spiritual 'keys'—a metaphorical representation of authority to open and shut spiritual doors across the nation. This authority allowed me to make decrees and take actions with significant spiritual implications.

My journey has been marked by a series of **Supernatural Confirmations** that underscored and supported my divine assignment. These confirmations came in various forms, such as repeated appearances of the number 222 and the reception of literal keys, symbolizing the spiritual authority I was being given. Each confirmation reinforced my mission and reminded me of the divine support backing my actions.

One of the most memorable and decisive actions I took was during a prayer outside the White House, which I describe as **A Bold Act at the White House.** Using the spiritual authority granted to me, I prayed fervently, making declarations that I believed would influence the course of the nation. This act of faith was not just symbolic but a real stance in the spiritual battle for the nation's future.

Throughout my journey, I have faced moments that tested my faith and resolve. One such moment occurred as I prayed in the cold outside the White House, feeling doubts about the impact of my prayers. However, an unexpected **Encounter That Reinforces Faith** with a stranger who recognized my work and affirmed the very scriptures I had been praying over, revitalized my spirit and confirmed that I was indeed following God's path. This encounter was a powerful reminder of the importance of steadfast faith and obedience in the face of adversity.

Finally, my ongoing mission, which I refer to as **Continued Mission Across America**, involves not just past actions but a current and active engagement in traveling the nation, praying, and proclaiming the need for revival. This continued mission is not a mere recounting of past deeds but an active, ongoing engagement in God's work across America. It represents a living, breathing movement that seeks to transform the nation through prayer and divine intervention.

Reflective Questions

1. How does the initial vision of riding with Christ shape Dutch's understanding of his purpose? How do visions or profound experiences shape your understanding of your own life's purpose?
2. What does this chapter teach about responding to divine calls to action? Reflect on a time when you felt called to take a significant step in faith.
3. In what ways does Dutch's story illustrate the concept of spiritual authority? How do you perceive and exercise spiritual authority in your own life?
4. How does Dutch's experience influence your view on the role of prayer in governmental or

national matters? Do you believe that prayer can change political outcomes?

5. Reflect on the incident where Dutch's faith was tested outside the White House. How do you respond when your faith or beliefs are tested in challenging circumstances?

Actionable Steps

1. **Cultivate** a Deeper Prayer Life: Develop a daily prayer routine that focuses not just on personal needs but also on broader issues such as national leadership, societal healing, and revival.

2. **Equip** Yourself with Biblical Knowledge: Study scriptures related to spiritual authority, such as Isaiah 22:22, to better understand and articulate your position and actions in the spiritual realm.

3. **Engage** in Community and National Matters: Start or participate in a prayer group that focuses on praying for your local community and nation, taking inspiration from Dutch's proactive approach to spiritual leadership.

JOURNALING Prompt

Reflect on a time when you felt a clear directive from God or a deep conviction to act on an issue. Journal about this experience, focusing on your initial reactions, how you responded, and what the outcomes were. Consider what this tells you about your readiness to follow divine guidance in the future.

THE RIDE

_____
_____
_____
_____
_____
_____
_____
_____
_____
_____
_____
_____
_____
_____
_____
_____
_____
_____
_____
_____
_____
_____
_____
_____
_____
_____

~

_____

_____

_____

_____

_____

_____

_____

_____

_____

_____

_____

_____

_____

_____

_____

_____

_____

_____

_____

_____

_____

_____

_____

_____

THE CALL

Embrace the call to intercession. It's a powerful tool that God uses to heal lands and peoples. Your prayers can build bridges and close gaps that divide.

"So I sought for a man among them who would make a wall, and stand in the gap before Me on behalf of the land, that I should not destroy it; but I found no one."
- Ezekiel 22:30, NKJV

In Chapter 2, "The Call," I explore the deep and vital role of intercession. Intercession is more than just praying; it's about standing in the gap, acting as a mediator between God and the people, and bringing about real change in our nation and our personal spiritual lives. This chapter is intended to help you understand and engage in this crucial task more effectively.

Intercession involves mediating, going between, and pleading on behalf of others, which is essential for understanding the depth and impact of what it means to intercede. **Defining Intercession** helps broaden our understanding of this practice—it's not just about offering prayers but about becoming a bridge that represents one party to another, often in significant spiritual and sometimes legal situations.

One of the key insights in this chapter is the Hebrew meaning of intercession, *paga*, which means "to meet." This shows that **The Power of 'Meeting' in Intercession** isn't just about the words we pray but about facilitating a meeting between God and the situation at hand. Through intercession, we invite God into the issues we face, not only meeting with Him in prayer but also confronting the powers of darkness. This dual meeting is crucial for spiritual breakthroughs.

The Role of Gatherings emphasizes why we gather in groups to pray. These aren't just regular meetings but strategic assemblies where God's people come together to seek His presence and intervention. These gatherings serve as a point of release for God's glory, allowing His voice and will to be more clearly perceived and followed within each state and across the nation.

Understanding the need for divine intervention leads us to appreciate why God is always **Seeking Intercessors**. Isaiah 59 highlights God's disappointment when He finds no one to stand for justice. This scripture underscores the essential role of intercessors as God's agents of justice and righteousness, who are called to stand in the gap where truth and morality have faltered.

In many spiritual landscapes, there are **'Gaps'** or breaches where sin and corruption have broken through God's protective boundaries. These gaps might appear as societal injustices, moral decay, or spiritual apathy. As intercessors, our role is to identify these breaches and spiritually stand in them, advocating for divine restoration and intervention.

The situation described in Ezekiel 22 provides a stark illustration of what happens when leaders fail to uphold their spiritual and moral duties—**Ezekiel's Example of Leadership and Holiness Violation**. This passage teaches us the critical need for integrity in leadership and the disastrous consequences when it is absent, highlighting the need for intercessors to pray fervently for our leaders.

From Ezekiel, we also learn the importance of someone willing to **Stand in the Gap**. When God searches for a person to stand before Him on behalf of the land, it's a profound calling. Those who respond to this call engage in a transformative process, not only for themselves but also for their communities and their nation. By standing in the gap, intercessors act as catalysts for divine intervention and change.

The overarching theme of this chapter emphasizes the **Transformative Impact of Intercession**. When we commit to standing in the gap, the spiritual shifts that occur can lead to tangible changes in the world around us. It is a powerful testament to the efficacy of living out our faith in very real and impactful ways.

Throughout the chapter, the narrative is woven with the idea that understanding and responding to the call of God is a **Progressive Understanding of God's Call**. This call is not static but dynamic, evolving as we grow in faith and obedience. It requires continual listening, learning, and adjusting as we align more closely with God's will.

Reflective Questions

1. How does the concept of intercession as a 'meeting' change your understanding of prayer and spiritual engagement?
2. Why is it important for believers to identify and stand in the 'gaps' within their communities and nations?

3. What lessons can be learned from Ezekiel 22 about the responsibilities of spiritual leaders?

4. In what ways does intercession affect not just spiritual realms but tangible, real-world situations?

5. How can understanding the progressive nature of God's call aid in your personal spiritual development?

Actionable Steps

1. **Cultivate a Regular Intercessory Practice**: Begin by setting aside dedicated time each day for intercession, focusing on specific 'gaps' you identify in your community or nation.

2. **Equip Yourself with Scriptural Insights on Intercession**: Study biblical examples of intercession, such as those found in Isaiah and Ezekiel, to deepen your understanding of your role as an intercessor.

3. **Engage with Intercessory Communities**: Join or form intercessory prayer groups that focus on specific issues or regions, enhancing your collective impact through shared insights and strengthened prayer.

Journaling Prompt

Reflect on a situation in your community or nation where you see a 'gap'—a place of need or brokenness. Journal about how you feel called to pray for this situation. What specific prayers might God be placing on your heart to help bridge this gap?

THE CALL

~

_____

_____

_____

_____

_____

_____

_____

_____

_____

_____

_____

_____

_____

_____

_____

_____

_____

_____

_____

_____

_____

_____

_____

_____

_____

_____

_____

_____

_____

CHAPTER 3
PLANTING THE HEAVENS

Embrace the call to intercession. It's a powerful tool that God uses to heal lands and peoples. Your prayers can build bridges and close gaps that divide.

"And I have put My words in your mouth; I have covered you with the shadow of My hand, that I may plant the heavens, lay the foundations of the earth, and say to Zion, 'You are My people'." - Isaiah 51:16, NKJV

In Chapter 3, "Planting the Heavens," I want to share with you the powerful role we have in speaking God's words into our world. This chapter explains how our words, like seeds, can bring about change in both the heavens and the earth. This idea comes from Isaiah 51:16, which tells us that God has put His words in our mouths so that we can plant the heavens and lay the foundations of the earth.

First, we must understand that **God's Words are Seeds**. Isaiah 51:16 reveals that God has placed His words in our mouths, likening them to seeds that can be planted in both the heavens and the earth. This metaphor shows the creative and transformative power of divine speech and our role in echoing it. When we speak God's words, we are planting seeds that can grow and bring about real change.

Our **Mouth as the Instrument of Planting** is crucial. The Hebrew word *peh*, meaning mouth, signifies not just a physical part of our body but also a spiritual instrument through which God's words are sounded forth into creation. This means our mouths have the power to shape reality by declaring God's truth, and it places a profound responsibility on us to speak life into various areas.

Prayers as Word Seeds is another important concept. When we pray, we are not just asking for things; we are planting seeds in the spiritual realm. These prayers can influence both heavenly and earthly contexts, showing that our words have significant power and potential. This idea expands the concept of prayer from mere requests to an act of spiritual planting that influences reality.

There is a spiritual battle to **Silence the Church's Voice**. The enemy wants to keep us from speaking God's words because he knows their power. Recognizing this tactic helps us understand the importance of speaking God's truth despite opposition. It's crucial for us to continue to speak God's words boldly, as part of a demon's assignment is to shut the mouth of Christ's Body. Too many in the Body of Christ have fallen into that error and embraced silence.

As God's heirs, we have a **Role in Planting**. We are entrusted with the continuation of His gardening, an ancient job that started with God Himself as the original Gardener. This means we are to speak life and order into the world, continuing God's original intent for His sons and daughters to declare His words onto the earth. He has put His Word in our mouths so that He may plant it in the heavens and on the earth.

I think about my grandfather when I talk about planting. He carefully chose and planted seeds every year, knowing they would grow into food for many people. This story of **Grandpa's Garden** shows how careful planting and tending can lead to abundant life, paralleling how we are to nurture the spiritual seeds we plant. Just as my grandfather's seeds planted a lot of gardens in

Waverly, Ohio, we, too, are to plant God's good word seeds into our cities and regions.

The **Biblical Foundation for Planting Words** shows that we are to speak God's words into the world to establish His kingdom principles. The scriptures provide a foundation for our role as planters of heavenly seeds, where God's words are sown into regions to bring about spiritual and societal alignment with His will. We are to declare the words of God into the heavens and the earth, mankind, nations, government, congregations, and people everywhere to set in place foundations for stable government and society.

The **Impact of Planted Words** is profound. Isaiah 55:11 promises that God's words will not return void but will accomplish what He desires. This means that when we speak God's words, they will bring about the change He intends. Foundations on the earth were established according to God's decreed word, and the condition of the heavens and the earth was dependent upon the Word of God, His spoken word, and it still is today.

Creation Through Words is a concept that goes back to the beginning of time when God created the world by speaking it into existence. Just as God created the universe through His spoken word, we are called to use our words to create and influence the spiritual and physical realms. The entire universe is made to hearken to the voice of God's Word, and heaven and earth are made to respond to the voice of God's Word. Angel armies are made to respond to the voice of God's Word, and human beings, made in God's image and likeness, are also carriers of God's voice when they are activated at the new birth.

Finally, by **Seeding the Atmosphere**, we can change the spiritual climate of regions and bring about spiritual awakening and reformation. By speaking God's word, we seed the spiritual atmosphere of regions, which can lead to spiritual awakening and reformation. This strategic planting can change the spiritual climate and bring about God's plans for those areas. When we speak God's words, we are planting seeds that can grow and transform the world around us.

This chapter emphasizes the immense power and responsibility we have as believers to use our words to plant the heavens and lay foundations on the earth, echoing God's creative work and bringing His kingdom to life in our surroundings.

Reflective Questions

1. How does understanding your words as seeds change the way you speak about your life, challenges, and aspirations?

2. In what ways can you actively combat the attempts to silence the Christian voice in your community or country?

3. What areas of your life need 'gardening'— where might you need to plant seeds of truth and hope?

4. Reflect on a time when you witnessed the powerful effect of God's word spoken in faith. What was the impact?

5. How can the concept of 'seeding the atmosphere' influence your approach to prayer and spiritual declaration?

Actionable Steps

1. **Cultivate a Habit of Speaking Life**: Regularly speak words of blessing, hope, and life over your circumstances, relationships, and challenges, recognizing the power of words to shape reality.

2. **Equip Yourself with Scripture**: Deepen your understanding of biblical declarations by studying verses that emphasize the power of the spoken word, and equip yourself to use Scripture effectively in your daily declarations.

3. **Engage in Strategic Spiritual Planting**:
   Actively participate in prayer gatherings or
   spiritual warfare efforts aimed at planting
   God's word in specific regions, communities,
   or situations needing divine intervention.

Journaling Prompt

Consider the areas in your life or community where negativity or despair seems to have taken root. How can you begin to 'plant' words of hope and faith in these areas? Journal about specific words or scriptures you can declare regularly to bring change.

~

_____

_____

_____

_____

_____

_____

_____

_____

_____

_____

_____

_____

_____

_____

_____

_____

_____

_____

_____

_____

_____

_____

_____

_____
_____
_____
_____
_____
_____
_____
_____
_____
_____
_____
_____
_____
_____
_____
_____
_____
_____
_____
_____
_____
_____
_____
_____
_____
_____
_____

CHAPTER 4
CAN A NATION BE RESTORED?

To understand God's full plan for your life, consider Acts 17:24-28. These verses explain that **God, who made everything, does not live in man-made temples. He doesn't need anything from us since He gives life to everyone. He made all nations from one blood and determined their times and places so they would seek Him and find Him. When we are in the right place at the right time, we can reach out to God and bring His blessings to earth. This starts the process of restoration, breaking old cycles and bringing us into God's perfect plan.**

S o, **Can a Nation Really Be Restored?** The Bible affirms this. In Isaiah 66:7-9, God says a nation can be born in a day. If God can do that, He can also change a nation that has gone astray. But restoration involves addressing issues like **illegal bloodshed, idolatry, immorality, and covenant breaking.** Acts 3:19-21 calls us to repent so that times of refreshing may come from the Lord, leading to the restoration of all things. Jesus left the Holy Spirit as His agent of reconciliation, restoring our ability to connect with God and working on every aspect of our lives.

Restoration in God's terms is not just about returning to a former state but involves multiplication. When God begins the process of restoration, it opens the door for exponential growth and fulfillment of His purposes. Our nation's foundation lies in the **United States Constitution and the Declaration of Independence**, highlighting our destiny to align with God's plan. Each state within the nation has a unique role and destiny that contributes to the whole.

For our nation to be transformed, **God's order must first be established in each state.** When strategic intercessors align with apostolic leaders, breakthrough begins. Intercessors carry God's burden, prophetic people make key declarations, and apostles set these decrees in motion. This alignment leads to significant spiritual breakthroughs and establishes God's will on earth.

A great example of this process occurred during the **Texas State Meeting**. The gathering started with reconciliation and progressed to prophetic declarations, revealing God's purposes and releasing His anointing over the state. The meeting in San Antonio included a powerful prophetic word from Dutch Sheets and declarations that addressed and corrected issues hindering God's plan for Texas.

Throughout the **50-State Tour**, the goal was to align the Body of Christ in each state with God's redemptive plan. This involved intercession, prophetic declarations, and apostolic execution. For example, during the meeting in Texas, **intercessory burdens** were lifted to God, leading to **revelation released**. This revelation was then followed by **prophetic declarations** and **apostolic execution**, culminating in divine fulfillment.

Worship and intercession play crucial roles in **tearing down snares** erected by the enemy and establishing God's will on earth. **Reconciliation follows repentance**, restoring friendship and fellowship with God. This principle was evident during the **50-State Tour**, where many states saw significant spiritual breakthroughs as they repented and reconciled with God's purposes.

Daniel's example shows us the power of prayer, fasting, and prophetic understanding. His dedication led to angelic visitation and revelation of the future, which helped him guide his people out of captivity. This pattern is essential for us today as we seek to align with God's will and bring about national restoration.

God is calling us to **shift and realign** with His perfect plan. This shift requires us to embrace an apostolic-sending mentality, allowing the Spirit of God to align us in His order. By overcoming obstacles and embracing repentance, we can move forward in God's purposes.

The restoration of a nation involves understanding **the importance of prophecy in our prayer lives**. Prophetic words are stored in Heaven until the right time, and when released, they bring about significant change. We must use these prophecies to war for our future, just as Daniel did.

By embracing God's wisdom, we can **dismantle demonic structures and overthrow thrones of iniquity**. The Ancient of Days, who holds all wisdom, grants us insight for present-day victory. As we seek Him intimately, He reveals hidden wisdom that transforms territories and releases captives.

In conclusion, **national restoration is possible** if we are willing to align with God's covenant blessing. This involves a shift from a discipling-teaching mentality to an apostolic-sending mentality, embracing God's order, and warring against the enemy's schemes. As we repent, reconcile, and align with God's purposes, we can see our nation realign and shift into God's plan.

REFLECTIVE QUESTIONS

1. What does it mean for you to be in the right place at the right time according to Acts 17:24-28?

2. How can addressing issues like illegal bloodshed, idolatry, immorality, and covenant breaking lead to national restoration?

3. Why is it important for each state to align with God's redemptive plan for the nation to be transformed?

4. How can worship and intercession play a role in tearing down snares erected by the enemy?

5. What can you learn from Daniel's example of prayer, fasting, and prophetic understanding for your personal spiritual growth?

ACTIONABLE STEPS

1. **Cultivate a Lifestyle of Repentance and Reconciliation:**

   - Regularly examine your heart and actions, asking God to reveal any areas where you need to repent.
   - Seek reconciliation in your relationships, making amends and restoring fellowship where needed.

1. **Equip Yourself with Prophetic Understanding:**

   - Study the prophetic words given to you and the scriptures to understand God's will for your life and community.
   - Join a community of believers who can help you grow in your prophetic gifting and understanding.

1. **Engage in Strategic Intercession:**

- Partner with others in prayer, focusing on specific needs and issues in your community and nation.
- Make prophetic declarations based on the revelation you receive, aligning your prayers with God's will.

Journaling Prompt

Reflect on a time when you experienced a significant shift in your spiritual journey. What led to that shift, and how did it align you more closely with God's will? How can you apply what you learned from that experience to your current spiritual walk?

CAN A NATION BE RESTORED?

_____

_____

_____

_____

_____

_____

_____

_____

_____

_____

_____

_____

_____

_____

_____

_____

_____

_____

_____

_____

_____

_____

_____

_____

_____

_____

_____

_____

~

_____

_____

_____

_____

_____

_____

_____

_____

_____

_____

_____

_____

_____

_____

_____

_____

_____

_____

_____

_____

_____

_____

_____

_____

_____

_____

_____

_____

THE ADJUSTMENT

"Embrace God's adjustments with a willing heart, knowing that each divine realignment brings you closer to His perfect plan for your life. As you submit to His corrections, you will experience healing, restoration, and the fulfillment of your God-given destiny."

"For I know the thoughts that I think toward you, says the Lord, thoughts of peace and not of evil, to give you a future and a hope." - Jeremiah 29:11 (NKJV)

I n Chapter 5, "The Adjustment," I share my journey through various life adjustments. Growing up, **the process of adjustment** began with my father, who used stern methods to shape my behavior and attitudes. My wife continued this trend, adjusting my thinking on things like communication and the number of shoes a woman needs. These experiences have made me realize how adjustments, whether minor or significant, contribute to our overall growth and understanding. It's a humorous but profound acknowledgment of how life shapes us through constant adjustments.

God as the ultimate Adjuster plays a significant role in our lives. Just as I experienced adjustments from people around me, God also adjusts our hearts, minds, and directions. These divine adjustments are essential for our personal and national restoration. When we align with His will, we open ourselves up to healing and restoration that only He can provide. God's adjustments are not just about correcting us but realigning us with His divine purpose.

Understanding **'katartizo'**, a Greek word meaning to adjust or put in its appropriate position, further emphasizes the need for alignment. This word appears in various biblical contexts, such as mending nets, repairing relationships, and restoring broken lives. It's about proper alignment, leading to healing and restoration. Just like mending a net or fixing a broken bone, our lives need to be properly aligned to function effectively.

Historical realignment is another crucial aspect. History often needs healing due to breaches like wars or broken relationships. Scriptures like Isaiah 58:12 and 2

Chronicles 7:14 talk about rebuilding ruins and healing lands through repentance, prayer, and seeking God. Healing these historical breaches is essential for restoring nations and individuals to their God-given destinies. We must address these past wounds to move forward effectively.

The **role of prophetic decrees** in bringing about divine adjustments cannot be overstated. Alongside prayer and fasting, these decrees help align individuals and nations with God's plans. Prophetic decrees are spiritual declarations that facilitate healing and restoration. They act as instruments through which God's will is pronounced and enacted in our lives and communities.

One notable example is **Tennessee's realignment**. God instructed me to tell Tennessee that He had broken a curse off the state that week, resulting in blessings. This was tied to the state's historical actions and recent support for Israel. When we shared this prophetic word, it was confirmed that Tennessee had indeed made a formal declaration to support Israel that very week. This validation increased faith and excitement, showing the tangible impact of prophetic words and actions in realigning a state with God's purposes.

Another example is **Michigan's recovery of its voice**. God revealed that Michigan had lost its prophetic voice due to historical alliances. A prophetic word led to the dismantling of these alliances and the restoration of the state's voice. Addressing past wrongs and restoring God's intended authority and influence is crucial for realignment. This process shows how spiritual actions can have significant, tangible impacts on regions.

The concept of **'abar'**, meaning to cross over or penetrate, is significant. This word denotes important transitions and covenantal acts, like Abraham crossing into a new land by God's instruction. Crossing over into new spiritual territories involves obedience and leads to covenantal blessings. Each generation must have its own crossing over, signifying a personal commitment to God's instructions and promises.

God's government and order are essential for experiencing new levels of His river—life, healing, and restoration. Embracing God's order is necessary for spiritual recovery and restoration. We must follow His divine patterns and order to experience deeper levels of His presence and blessings. This acceptance is crucial for unlocking new dimensions of spiritual growth and healing.

Looking at **the future of America**, I envision a great awakening where spiritual adjustments lead to national revival and blessings. This involves a collective crossing over into God's purposes, resulting in widespread revival. America's destiny is tied to a spiritual reawakening and realignment with God's plans, leading to the breaking of curses and the release of blessings. It's a powerful vision of what can happen when a nation turns back to God.

In conclusion, these adjustments and realignments, both personal and national, are vital for fulfilling our God-given destinies. As we embrace these changes, we open ourselves to God's healing, restoration, and blessings. It's a privilege to partner with Him in this transformative journey.

Reflective Questions

1. How have personal adjustments in your life prepared you for spiritual realignment?
2. In what ways have you experienced God as the ultimate Adjuster in your life?
3. What historical breaches in your personal or family history might need healing and realignment?
4. How can prophetic decrees and prayers play a role in your spiritual journey and alignment?
5. What steps can you take to align more closely with God's government and order in your life?

ACTIONABLE STEPS

1. **Cultivate Awareness:**

- Identify Areas of Adjustment: Regularly examine areas in your life that need God's adjustment.
- Journal Your Adjustments: Keep a journal to record moments of divine adjustment.
- Stay Humble: Approach each day with a humble heart, ready to receive God's adjustments.

1. **Equip Yourself with God's Word:**

- Study Biblical Examples: Delve into Scripture to understand how God adjusts individuals and nations.
- Memorize Key Verses: Commit verses about alignment and God's adjustments to memory.
- Engage in Prophetic Decrees: Practice making prophetic declarations over your life and community.

1. **Engage in Spiritual Practices:**

- Pray for Realignment: Regularly pray for personal and national alignment with God's will.
- Participate in Fasting: Incorporate fasting as a spiritual discipline.
- Join a Community: Engage with a community committed to prayer, prophetic decrees, and seeking God's alignment.

JOURNALING **Prompt**

Reflect on a recent adjustment you felt God made in your life. How did it change your perspective or direction? Write about the experience and any insights or revelations you gained from it.

~

_____

_____

_____

_____

_____

_____

_____

_____

_____

_____

_____

_____

_____

_____

_____

_____

_____

_____

_____

_____

_____

_____

_____

_____

_____

CHAPTER 6

CONNECTING WITH HEAVEN AND EARTH

Embrace God's adjustments with a willing heart,
knowing that each divine realignment brings you closer
to His perfect plan for your life. As you submit to His
corrections, you will experience healing, restoration, and
the fulfillment of your God-given destiny.

**"For I know the thoughts that I think toward you,
says the Lord, thoughts of peace and not of evil, to
give you a future and a hope."** - Jeremiah 29:11 (NKJV)

I n Chapter 6, "Connecting with Heaven and Earth,"
I explore the significance of the unseen realm of
the spirit and how it impacts our lives and
destinies. **There is a relatively unknown dimension
that must be understood** to fully partner with God and

experience His blessings. This invisible realm is real and active, influencing much of what happens on earth. It controls the destinies of people and nations, and understanding it helps us partner with God more effectively.

Most people, including Christians, give little thought to this unseen world that governs the one we see. Our culture, which emphasizes education and intellectualism, often makes us skeptical of this invisible activity. But the Bible is filled with descriptions and accounts of this spiritual dimension. Without it, there would be no God, satan, angels, demons, fall of humankind, birth of Christ, redemption through the cross, miracles, or resurrection of the dead. Many Christians live without considering how much this realm affects us, missing out on the opportunity to influence it.

Yet here is an important truth: The more we learn to function in the invisible realm of the spirit, recognizing and applying its principles, the more we can partner with God, positively impact our world, avoid the snares of the evil one, and enjoy the blessings of our salvation. This was the primary purpose of our 50-State Tour. By understanding this dimension, we can see how the spiritual realm affects our natural world.

One example is the story of the **Amalekites defeated before an invisible force** in Exodus 17:8-16. Moses, Aaron, and Hur went up on a hill above the battlefield while Joshua and the army fought below. When Moses held up the staff of God, Israel prevailed, but when he grew tired and lowered it, Amalek began to dominate. Aaron and Hur helped Moses keep the staff raised, ensuring Israel's victory. The staff represented God's power and authority. Raising it symbolized relying on God's strength, while lowering it meant fighting in their strength. This story shows how actions in the visible realm can activate God's invisible power, determining the outcome in the visible realm.

Another example is the story of **unseen allies** found in 2 Kings 6:8-23. The king of Aram sent an army to kill Elisha, and when Elisha's servant saw the army, he panicked. Elisha, seeing into the spirit realm, reassured him that they had more allies than enemies. He prayed for God to open his servant's eyes, revealing a host of angelic forces that struck the enemy with blindness. This story demonstrates how the invisible realm controls events in the visible world and how spiritual forces can aid us.

Heavenly combat is illustrated in Daniel 10:10-21. Daniel sought insight from God for 21 days, and when an angel finally arrived with the answer, he explained that he had been delayed by the prince of the kingdom of Persia until Michael, a chief prince, helped him. This story shows that battles in the spiritual realm can affect what happens on earth, emphasizing the need for spiritual awareness and persistence in prayer.

We must learn to partner with Heaven to experience spiritual breakthroughs. This involves recognizing the spiritual activities around us and intentionally operating in the spiritual realm by obeying biblical principles and seeking God's guidance. Before the Tour, God had been teaching me about this dimension. By studying the five references to "heavenly places" in Ephesians, I saw a powerful sequence of verses. These verses reveal that we have been given everything we need to operate in the spiritual realm, sharing in Christ's authority. The Church is called to manifest God's wisdom to opposing spiritual forces and overcome them using God's power.

The Lord emphasized the necessity of operating more effectively in this spiritual dimension. Matthew 16:18-19 describes the Church's authority to govern in the spiritual realm, binding and loosing spiritual forces from earth. This passage teaches that our actions on earth can influence the spiritual realm, and vice versa. Jesus gave us the keys to the Kingdom of Heaven, promising that the powers of hell would not overpower us when we use this authority.

God also led me to Micah 2:13, which refers to the Lord as "the Breaker" who goes before us. The word "up" in this verse means to ascend or rise up, indicating that we must follow Christ into the heavenly places to experience breakthroughs. **Breaking through in the invisible realm of the spirit always creates breakthrough in the visible, natural realm**.

During the Tour, the Holy Spirit gave me a powerful lesson about connecting Heaven and earth. In Oklahoma, Chuck prophesied about God opening a door, and the Holy Spirit revealed that this was a spiritual occurrence in the heavens. He taught me to go through spiritual doors in the heavenly realm before seeing the results on earth. **Connecting Heaven and earth releases God's glory**, bringing realignment, restoration, healing, and the release of His presence and power.

The release of God's glory is significant. Moses cried out for it in Exodus 33:18. The Hebrew word "kabowd" means "weighty" or "heavy," signifying authority and prosperity. When Heaven and earth connect, God's glory is felt, and great authority is released. The New Testament word "doxa" means recognizing something or someone for what they truly are. When God's glory is released, He is recognized, and His presence changes everything.

One remarkable example of this connection is the **capture of Saddam Hussein**. During the Tour, Chuck received a word from the Lord and prophesied Saddam's capture within seven days. We prayed and decreed his capture, and three days later, Saddam was found. This event demonstrates the power of connecting Heaven and earth through prayer and declaration, leading to tangible results on earth.

We must learn to partner with the invisible forces of God. There are more for us than against us, and we need to understand the ways of the spirit to draw from this invisible world. If we do, our nation will continue to turn back to God, breakthroughs will occur, and another great awakening will unfold.

Join us in this worthy and eternal cause!

Reflective Questions

1. How can you become more aware of the unseen realm in your daily life?
2. In what ways have you experienced the influence of the spiritual realm?
3. How can you intentionally operate in the spiritual realm?
4. What role do prophetic decrees play in your spiritual journey?
5. How can you better partner with Heaven to experience breakthroughs?

ACTIONABLE STEPS

1. **Cultivate Awareness**

- Recognize the Unseen Realm: Be mindful of the spiritual dimension and its influence on your life.
- Journal Spiritual Encounters: Keep a record of moments when you sense spiritual activity or intervention.
- Seek God's Guidance: Regularly pray for insight and understanding of the spiritual realm.

1. **Equip Yourself with God's Word**

- Study Biblical Examples: Learn from Scripture about the unseen realm and how to engage with it.
- Memorize Key Verses: Commit to memory verses that emphasize the spiritual dimension and our authority in Christ.
- Declare God's Promises: Practice speaking God's promises and truths over your life and circumstances.

1. **Engage in Spiritual Practices**

- Pray and Fast: Regularly engage in prayer and fasting to seek God's guidance and breakthrough.
- Worship and Praise: Incorporate worship as a way to connect with the spiritual realm and invite God's presence.
- Join a Faith Community: Engage with a community of believers who support and encourage your spiritual growth.

Journaling Prompt

Reflect on a recent experience where you felt the influence of the spiritual realm. How did it impact your perspective or actions? Write about the experience and any insights you gained from it.

~

_____

_____

_____

_____

_____

_____

_____

_____

_____

_____

_____

_____

_____

_____

_____

_____

_____

_____

_____

_____

_____

_____

_____

_____

_____

_____

_____

_____

_____

_____

_____

_____

_____

_____

_____

_____

_____

_____

_____

_____

_____

_____

_____

_____

_____

_____

_____

_____

_____

_____

_____

_____

_____

_____

_____

_____

_____

CHAPTER 7

RECEIVING THE ANOINTING TO STAND STRONG - UNDERSTANDING THE ISSACHAR ANOINTING

You are an important part of God's plan. Embrace the Issachar anointing, which helps you understand God's timing and seasons. By recognizing His timing, you can align yourself with His purposes and experience the fullness of His blessings. Trust in God's sovereignty, timing, and placement to fulfill your destiny. As you align with His purposes, you will experience breakthroughs and witness His Kingdom advancing on earth.

Fear not, for I am with you; be not dismayed, for I am your God. I will strengthen you, yes, I will help you, I will uphold you with My righteous right hand. ... Those who war against you shall be as nothing.... Fear not, I will help you (Isaiah 41:10,12-13 NKJV).

Understanding the times and seasons is crucial for victory in our personal lives and territories. This concept, which I refer to as the **Issachar anointing**, means recognizing God's timing and knowing how to respond. When God called Dutch and me to visit all 50 states, we felt an urgency to accomplish His will. While God is sovereign and capable of doing everything Himself, He created us to cultivate and watch over His creation. Just as Abraham had to leave Ur of the Chaldees and go to Canaan, we too have specific places and seasons where we must serve and reflect our faith.

God's sovereignty includes placing us in specific times and locations. **God determines times and seasons** for our lives, and we are set in a sequence within His plan on earth. We must seek Him during our appointed times. Understanding this helps us align with His purposes and experience His blessings.

Chronos refers to general time, while kairos refers to the opportune or strategic time. **Kairos is an extension of chronos**. God's plans unfold through chronological time, leading to opportune moments. Our faithfulness in chronos allows us to enter kairos, where strategic opportunities arise. This process culminates in pleroo, the fullness of time when God's purposes are fully realized. Like a woman giving birth, we go through stages of development, labor, and finally the fullness of new life.

The Issachar anointing is essential for advancing in victory. **The Issachar anointing** helps us understand the timing of God and know what to do. The sons of Issachar were known for their understanding of the times and their ability to discern what Israel should do. This anointing involves recognizing God's timing, carrying His burdens, and releasing His blessings at the right moment.

God's timing is often connected to the Feasts in the Old Testament. **The timing element in the Word of God** revolves around these feasts, which help us understand His purposes on earth. By aligning with God's calendar, we can better recognize His plans and move forward in His will. The Hebrew Year 5762 marked a seven-year war season, illustrating the importance of discerning the times and seasons.

Prophetic declarations and apostolic proclamations are powerful tools. **Decreeing, declaring, and proclaiming God's will** brings His purposes to earth. By hearing from God and speaking His words, we unlock miracles and release blessings. Throughout the 50-State Tour, we made declarations to align states with God's will, believing that these proclamations would bring transformation.

We must learn to stand and withstand in spiritual

warfare. **Stand and withstand** by putting on the whole armor of God. Ephesians 6:10-18 teaches us to be strong in the Lord and stand against the schemes of the devil. By submitting to God and resisting the enemy, we can overcome spiritual battles.

To stand and withstand, we need the anointing. **Be anointed** with the Holy Spirit to accomplish your assigned tasks. The anointing breaks the yoke and empowers us for victory. Whether it's receiving physical refreshment, restoring vision, or breaking curses, the anointing equips us for God's purposes.

The 50-State Tour demonstrated the power of prophetic and apostolic ministry. **We must keep going** and advance God's Kingdom. Identify apostolic leaders, embrace new opportunities, and be willing to shift from maintenance to dominion. By watching signs on earth and identifying ripe fields for Kingdom invasion, we can bring transformation to our communities.

God's sovereignty, timing, and placement are central to fulfilling His will. **Trust in His divine timing and placement** to receive the anointing needed to stand strong and fulfill your destiny. As you align with His purposes, you will experience breakthroughs, and His Kingdom will advance on earth.

Reflective Questions

1. How can you become more aware of God's timing and seasons in your life?
2. In what areas do you need to trust God's placement and timing more?
3. How can you cultivate the Issachar anointing in your life?
4. What role do prophetic declarations play in your spiritual journey?
5. How can you prepare to stand and withstand in spiritual warfare?

ACTIONABLE STEPS

1. **Cultivate Awareness**

- Recognize God's Timing: Be mindful of the seasons and times God has set for your life.
- Journal Spiritual Insights: Keep a record of moments when you sense God's timing and guidance.
- Seek God's Wisdom: Regularly pray for discernment and understanding of the times.

1. **Equip Yourself with God's Word:**

- Study Biblical Examples: Learn from Scripture about the Issachar anointing and God's timing.
- Memorize Key Verses: Commit to memory verses that emphasize God's sovereignty and timing.
- Declare God's Promises: Practice speaking God's promises and truths over your life and circumstances.

1. **Engage in Spiritual Practices**

- Pray and Fast: Regularly engage in prayer and fasting to seek God's guidance and breakthrough.
- Worship and Praise: Incorporate worship as a way to connect with God and invite His presence.
- Join a Faith Community: Engage with a community of believers who support and encourage your spiritual growth.

Journaling Prompt

Reflect on a recent experience where you felt God's

timing and placement in your life. How did it impact your perspective or actions? Write about the experience and any insights you gained from it.

~

_____

_____

_____

_____

_____

_____

_____

_____

_____

_____

_____

_____

_____

_____

_____

_____

_____

_____

_____

_____

_____

_____

_____

~

_____

_____

_____

_____

_____

_____

_____

_____

_____

_____

_____

_____

_____

_____

_____

_____

_____

_____

_____

_____

_____

_____

_____

_____

CHAPTER 8
TIME CATCHES UP WITH THE DECREE

Trust in God's timing. Though you may not see immediate results, remember that God's plans unfold perfectly. Stay faithful and patient, knowing that He is working all things for your good.

"For I know the plans that I have for you," declares the Lord, "plans for prosperity and not for disaster, to give you a future and a hope." (Jeremiah 29:11 NASB)

When Chuck and I arrived in Alaska, we didn't know what message we would share. Chuck always made me go first, joking that he'd get his part while I was speaking. This pattern worked because when I began to preach under a prophetic anointing, his strong prophetic gift would engage, revealing much about the state. In Alaska, Chuck attended a prayer meeting before I arrived and shared that God called Alaska His "alpha and omega state." Although I didn't understand it at first, God soon revealed its meaning to me.

Alaska is an initiating state. The term "Alpha and Omega" from Revelation 22:13, a title of Christ, means "the first and the last, the beginning and the end." God showed us that Alaska was to be a state of beginnings, a place to initiate His purposes. For instance, the modern prayer movement in America and beyond was greatly influenced by Alaska's early prayer initiatives, largely led by Mary Glazier and her group, Intercessors for Alaska.

God also revealed a hindrance to this calling through Alaska's geography. An island west of the mainland is part of Alaska but lies on the other side of the International Date Line. Traveling to the island moves you into tomorrow, while traveling back to the mainland moves you into yesterday. This unique geography symbolizes Christ's eternal nature and His ability to exist in yesterday, today, and tomorrow simultaneously.

We can always move forward. However, God showed me that Alaska's ability to represent Christ as the Alpha and Omega was hindered by a cycle of getting stuck in the past. This meant that whenever God tried to move them into new truth (tomorrow), they would revert to the old (yesterday). This pattern needed to be broken for them to fulfill their calling as pioneers of new spiritual movements.

This message is relevant to all of us. **God wants to reveal His purposes, expose the enemy's tactics, and give us strategies for recovery and fulfillment.** His desire is that our "latter" days be greater than our "former" days (Haggai 2:9). Even if we face setbacks, we can always move forward if we listen to and obey Him.

As part of this revelation in Alaska, the Holy Spirit highlighted Isaiah 46:10 and Jeremiah 29:11. **The word "end" and "future" come from the same Hebrew word, achariyth.** This word can mean "after," "later," "behind," or "following." It illustrates the Hebrew way of thinking, like a man rowing a boat backward into the future. While we may not see what's ahead, we trust that God has declared our destiny from the beginning. This concept reminds us that our future and destiny are secure in God's hands.

As I meditated on Isaiah 46:10, the Holy Spirit impressed on me that **time catches up with God's decree.** When God reveals His intentions for our lives, it may take years for them to come to pass. Like Abraham, who waited 25 years for Isaac, and David, who waited 20 years to become king, we must keep rowing by faith into our future. Despite the long wait, we can trust that time will eventually catch up with God's decree.

In 1973, I had an experience where the Holy Spirit spoke to me about my future. He revealed aspects of my calling and anointing that are only now beginning to unfold. **We must remember that God often speaks far in advance of fulfillment.** As we continue to row by faith, we will eventually row into our destiny, just as Alaska did.

Chuck and I often asked God, "What are You saying to this state right now?" **Decreeing the decree** means agreeing with and declaring what God has said about us. As we align with His plans, we release the creative power of His word, causing His purposes to be established.

Receive the Holy Spirit's help in discerning the times and seasons. The sons of Issachar were known for their ability to understand the times and know what to do (1 Chronicles 12:32). We, too, must seek this ability to discern the Spirit's timings. With the Holy Spirit's guidance, our latter days can be greater than our former. Keep rowing—time will catch up with His decree for you!

Reflective Questions

1. How can you apply the concept of rowing into your future by faith in your current situation?

2. What areas of your life are you struggling to move forward from the past? How can you break free from these cycles?

3. How do you discern the timings of the Spirit in your personal life?

4. What are some promises or decrees God has given you that you are still waiting to see fulfilled?

5. How can you better align with God's plans and purposes for your life?

Actionable Steps

Cultivate a habit of seeking God's guidance daily to understand His timing and purposes for your life.

Equip yourself with knowledge of Scripture and the Holy Spirit's voice to discern His will and direction.

Engage in prayer and prophetic declaration, speaking God's promises over your life and circumstances.

JOURNALING **Prompt**

Reflect on a time when you felt God gave you a

promise or direction for your life. How did you respond, and what steps can you take to align more closely with His timing and purposes now? Write about your journey of faith and any insights the Holy Spirit reveals to you about moving forward into your destiny.

TIME CATCHES UP WITH THE DECREE

~

_____
_____
_____
_____
_____
_____
_____
_____
_____
_____
_____
_____
_____
_____
_____
_____
_____
_____
_____
_____
_____
_____
_____
_____

CHAPTER 9
THE REIGNING CHURCH

When Jesus asked His disciples who they thought He was, Peter answered, "You are the Christ, the Son of the living God." Jesus then declared that upon this revelation, He would build His church (ekklesia), and the gates of hell would not prevail against it. He also gave us the authority to bind and loose on earth as it is in heaven (Matthew 16:13-19).

As sons and daughters of God, we are commanded to forbid or permit things on earth. This comes from God's original intent for His people to reign with Him and exercise dominion. The church is meant to be involved in government, reflecting Jesus' Kingdom. Jesus first established His Kingdom and then introduced His church. For nearly three years, He preached about the Kingdom, saying, "Repent, for the Kingdom of Heaven is at hand."

Understanding Kingdom is essential before we can understand the church. The Kingdom is a ruling and reigning branch of Christ's spiritual Kingdom on earth. Jesus' Kingdom is real but unseen, affecting the visible world. The message of the Kingdom has been minimized, and Christ's intent for His church to rule has been distorted. Most believers have been taught the opposite, influenced by hell's efforts to suppress this truth.

A Kingdom worldview is necessary for fulfilling the dominion mandate and the Great Commission. Without it, Christianity cannot function as intended. Jesus didn't establish a dormant Kingdom but one that expects His influence to change cultures through His followers' actions. The church must act according to His Word, forbidding and permitting as He directs.

The Greek word for "kingdom," **basileia**, means royal dominion and the realm of a king. Jesus is King over heaven and earth, ruling everywhere, including hell. His authority is boundless, and He expects His Kingdom's church, His body, to exercise this authority on earth. As **heirs of God and joint-heirs with Christ**, we are to rule with Him now, not just in the future.

Jesus preached the Kingdom before introducing the church. His first sermon in Galilee focused on the Kingdom, and He continued to preach about it, demonstrating its presence by healing the sick and casting out demons. The Kingdom is here, not just a future reality. He trained His disciples to understand and declare the Kingdom's presence.

Christ's church is part of His Kingdom on earth. The word Jesus used for church, **ekklesia**, is a political, judicial, and governmental term, reflecting a ruling body. It means "an assembly of citizens summoned for a purpose." This assembly had the authority to make laws, appoint officials, decide on policies, rule on treason, and even summon the army.

The **ekklesia** is not a religious word or a place of worship. It's an assembly of people with authority. The first English Bible translation to use "church" instead of "ekklesia" was the Geneva New Testament in 1557. The word "church" was influenced by religious hierarchies, but it's crucial to understand what Jesus meant by ekklesia: a governing body with legislative authority.

Jesus said His **ekklesia would have the final decision** on laws and governance. They were to be involved in shaping culture, education, laws, and societal standards. The ekklesia was to ensure that cultural values aligned with God's Word. They were to judge corruption, appoint officials, and remove those who did not uphold biblical principles.

A governing body, the ekklesia had the power to replace corrupt leaders and ensure righteous governance. Thayer's Greek Lexicon defines ekklesia as an assembly convened for deliberation, responsible for cultural standards and laws. Christians are to raise their hands, vote, and publicly decide on leaders and policies, ensuring they align with God's Word.

The **Romans also had ekklesias** to govern conquered territories, shaping culture and administering laws to make regions resemble Rome. Jesus used this term intentionally, knowing its implications. His ekklesia is to be the governing body of His Kingdom, representing His authority on earth.

Every kingdom has distinct areas: a king, geographical boundaries, laws, a society, a government, and an economy. Jesus' Kingdom has all these, and His ekklesia is to steward them on earth. The church is to ensure biblical laws, societal values, and ethical financial behavior.

Apostle Joseph Mattera describes the ekklesia as the **"new congress of His kingdom."** Jesus calls His followers to rule with Him, shaping culture and governance according to His Word. The church is to be involved in politics, legislation, and cultural decisions, acting as Jesus' congress on earth.

Read Candice's story as an example of answering

God's call to influence culture and governance. She ran for public office, mobilized the church, and won, demonstrating the power of God's ekklesia in action.

Jesus' use of ekklesia calls the church to **shape culture, influence public policy, and ensure biblical standards**. The church is to speak against corruption, legislate righteousness, and transform territories. We are authorized in Jesus' name to fulfill this mandate.

While we won't have a perfect world until Jesus returns, we can impact governments and cultures now. We are expected to do so as Christ's ekklesia, ruling and reigning with Him on earth.

Reflective Questions

1. How can you exercise your authority as part of Christ's ekklesia in your community?
2. What steps can you take to ensure your actions align with a Kingdom worldview?
3. In what ways can you influence public policy and governance according to biblical principles?
4. How can you support and encourage others in your church to engage in cultural and political issues?

5. What specific areas of your life need alignment with the principles of Christ's Kingdom?

Actionable Steps

Cultivate a deeper understanding of the Kingdom of God by studying Scripture and seeking revelation from the Holy Spirit.

Equip yourself and others with knowledge about the authority and responsibilities of Christ's ekklesia, encouraging active involvement in cultural and political matters.

Engage in your community by participating in local governance, voting, and advocating for policies that align with biblical principles.

Journaling Prompt

Reflect on your role as part of Christ's ekklesia. How can you actively participate in shaping culture and governance according to God's Word? Write about specific steps you can take to influence your community and support others in doing the same.

_____
_____
_____
_____
_____
_____
_____
_____
_____
_____
_____
_____
_____
_____
_____
_____
_____
_____
_____
_____
_____
_____
_____
_____
_____
_____
_____

$\sim$

_____

_____

_____

_____

_____

_____

_____

_____

_____

_____

_____

_____

_____

_____

_____

_____

_____

_____

_____

_____

_____

_____

_____

_____

_____

_____

CHAPTER 10

DECLARATIONS AND DECREES FOR THE NATION

We are in a crucial time for our nation, a season of transformation and divine intervention. God's purposes are unfolding, and His promises are being fulfilled. We must align ourselves with His will, making decrees that will bring about change and manifest His Kingdom on earth. Remember, we are not alone in this mission; angel armies are activated to assist us. Let us stand firm, declare His word, and watch as He brings revival and restoration to our land.

Isaiah 55:11 (NKJV): "So shall My word be that goes forth from My mouth; it shall not return to Me void, but it shall accomplish what I please, and it shall prosper in the thing for which I sent it."

I n this chapter, we decree that the United States has reconnected to its covenant roots and has entered a God-ordained season of reset. We believe we are in days of change with angel armies activated to help fulfill His purposes, including U-Turns, Turnarounds, and Boomerang Strategies. These heavenly interventions ensure that hell will not stop God's plans. As we journey through this season, we see a **glorious remnant mobilizing**, using their decrees to engage angel armies, as stated in Isaiah 55:11: "The words that come out of my mouth will not come back empty-handed. They'll do the work I sent them to do, they'll complete the assignment I gave them."

We declare that we are in days of **awakening and revival**, with a call for an acceleration of anointing and outpourings, supported by angel armies dedicated to revival. We decree that **America will be saved**, and we extend this hope to all nations, affirming that it is time for global salvation. There will be no more delays as **revival comes**. We proclaim that **dry bones will live again**, with new breath entering God's people, causing them to unite and stand as a great army. **Re-vive-all angels** will refresh us for this season, reviving everything that has been dormant.

In this time, we decree that angels are stirring the

waters, leading to accelerated **healings and miracles**. The harvest is now, with prodigals returning, new converts joining the faith, and a billion-soul harvest manifesting as prophesied. Angels will assist in this great harvest, as mentioned in Matthew 13:39: "The harvest is the end of the age, and the reapers are the angels." As we prepare for this influx, we expect that when the King comes in, **everything changes**. We look for God to reign over our lives and our nation.

Justice will prevail over injustice, with the Ekklesia rising to use their voice and authority to shake down demon principalities and powers. We declare that **evil decrees will not succeed** in our nation, as powers of darkness will fall, and thrones of iniquity will not stand. The battle is the Lord's, and He does not lie. We bind the Baal stronghold over our nation and proclaim that the Naphtali generation is coming forth to stand against societal and cultural sins, as highlighted in Deuteronomy 27:13.

We proclaim a **new backbone in the Ekklesia**, with strong, vital, and courageous individuals rising who will not back down. Every confinement is broken off, and angels are released to advance God's Kingdom. God's promise of **break up, break out, and breakthrough** will be fulfilled, and an anointing to prevail is being released. Doors to new areas, opportunities, places, and lands are opening, and God is making a way through. We are called to pass over and possess these new territories.

As we raise the bar, we receive **fresh vision and increased anointing**. A new Pentecost, greater than the outpouring in the book of Acts, is upon us, enabling us to function in a Holy Spirit-planned purpose for the decades to come. The barren places will become fruitful, and the arrow of the Lord's deliverance has been released from Heaven. We will experience fresh anointing, outpourings of the Holy Spirit, and increased angel activity.

We decree that **ancient wells are opening** and that the capped wells of evangelism will be uncapped. New roads, inroads, mantles, visions, and new harvests are being declared in the name of Jesus. This is the era when the Ekklesia sits on the throne of their regions, influencing the natural realms of earth through the spiritual Kingdom. A move of God has begun and cannot be stopped. We declare a breaking of hope deferred, replacing it with supernatural hope and strength.

We decree the sound of an **abundance of rain and revival** affecting every generation. America shall be saved. Angels are assisting fivefold ministries to overcome darkness in their regions. The Kingdom of Christ Jesus is growing and expanding its influence in all 50 states. God is doing new things, and now they will spring forth. The church will rise and be the salt and light Jesus said it would be. Promises, faith decrees, dreams, and visions of the Holy Spirit are activating in our nation. Those who have sat in great darkness will now live in great light.

We proclaim that **angels of breakthrough** are working with the heirs of God to break oppression from the land and release freedom. The angel gate of Heaven is open over this nation, and angel armies are aligning us with our covenants with God. The greatest days are not in our past—they are in our present and future. Supernatural recovery is coming for all lost inheritance, and every promise God has made will grow and produce its fruit. No weapons formed against us will prosper. Our God will anoint us to defeat them. The gifts of the Holy Spirit will function at higher levels than the church has ever seen before, assisting in harvest evangelism. The true Ekklesia is moving from glory to glory to glory.

We decree that the assignments in prophetic words will accelerate to fullness and not one will return empty. Waves of Kingdom revival will surge around the world, and hell cannot stop it. Rebel government will be purged from the land, and God will raise up leaders who have His heart. Evil ones are being dethroned, displaced, and removed. The world will see a mighty, bold, New Testament Church in this era, and it begins with me. Favor, favor, favor—open doors orchestrated by the Holy Spirit, and angel armies will accompany us to achieve decrees that have been planned by God. There are more with us than against us; by the power of His Spirit and in His name, we win. The Holy Spirit is bringing order into the disorder of this world, and an innumerable number of angels are activating to help us. The Ekklesia will now deploy, and the roots of hell will wither and die, scatter and shatter. God's calvary, the chariots of fire, will help us win great victories. The release of government angels will assist the Ekklesia to reign with Christ. The arrow of the Lord's deliverance will hit the mark.

Reflective Questions

1. How can you align your personal prayers with the decrees mentioned in this chapter?
2. What specific areas in your life need revival and a fresh outpouring of the Holy Spirit?
3. In what ways can you actively participate in bringing justice to your community?
4. How can you cultivate a new backbone of courage and strength in your spiritual walk?
5. What steps can you take to ensure that you are a part of the glorious remnant mobilizing for God's purposes?

Actionable Steps

Cultivate: Develop a daily habit of declaring God's promises over your life and nation. Speak life into every situation, believing that His word will not return void.

Equip: Equip yourself with knowledge of God's word and His promises. Study scriptures related to revival, justice, and God's Kingdom to strengthen your faith and understanding.

Engage: Engage in community activities that promote justice and righteousness. Be a voice for the voiceless and stand against injustice in your local area.

JOURNALING **Prompt**

Reflect on a time when you experienced a breakthrough after a period of prayer and declaration. How did it change your perspective on the power of decreeing God's word? What specific areas in your life or community can you begin to decree change over today? Write down your thoughts and commit to daily declarations.

IGNITING THE FLAMES OF FAITH

Faith and Flame Press is a Christian book publishing company that is passionate about igniting the flames of faith in the hearts of readers around the world. Our mission is to publish books that inspire, enlighten, and uplift the spirit, and help readers deepen their understanding of their faith and spirituality.

At Faith and Flame Press, we believe that books have the power to transform lives and to shape the world we live in. That's why we are committed to publishing books that are not only spiritually uplifting but also intellectually stimulating, well-researched, and thought-provoking.

Made in United States
North Haven, CT
01 September 2024

56835330R00059